Bongo Basics

By Claire Goddard

Copyright © 2016 Claire Goddard

All Rights Reserved

Contents

INTRODUCTION	5
BUYING A BONGO	6
CONVERSION OPTIONS	11
ACCESS ALL AREAS (GETTING IN AND OUT)	16
GETTING READY FOR THE OFF	24
DRIVING AN AUTOMATIC	26
SWITCHES AND BUTTONS	36
WARNING / DISPLAY LIGHTS	58
QUIRKY BONGO BITS	67
ACCESSORIES	72
FREQUENTLY ASKED QUESTIONS	91
WHAT NOW?	100
NOTE FROM THE AUTHOR	102

Introduction

This book covers all things Bongo and Freda (Mazda Bongos and Ford Freda's are the same vehicle just with a different badge). It is a collection of the useful bits and bobs you need to know and will hopefully answer all of those questions you have.

If you are yet to embark upon your Bongo journey there is a section covering the types of conversions you can choose from and what you need to look out for before parting with your cash.

If you have just purchased your first Bongo this book will guide you through all the aspects of your campervan from what button does what to accessing the engine and everything in-between.

I have added in some useful website addresses here and there and you can also check out my You Tube channel Bongo-ing Mad. Here you will find video demonstrations and guides that will help bring the book to life.

You can also find me on Facebook (Bongo-ing Mad) so why not Like my page and keep up to date with all the latest Bongo news.

Buying a Bongo

As well as considering if you should buy an unconverted or converted Bongo (check out the later chapter) and, if so, which one, it's also worth looking out for the following:

Rust
As Bongos were made in Japan they are not designed to deal with the damage that salt used on our roads in winter can cause; in Japan they prefer to use winter tyres. They can therefore be prone to rusting underneath. They also rust around the rear wheel arches as internal condensation pools here. Ask if the van has been under sealed as this protects from rust.

Check any Bongo you are considering purchasing for signs of rust and always ask to look at any MOT advisories as these will highlight any serious rust underneath that you may not be able to see.

NOTE:

It is rare to find a Bongo without any form of rust even if only very minor due to the age of the vehicles. Always treat rust to avoid it spreading.

Coolant Issues / Head Gasket
According to Practical Motorhome the Bongo is best known for its head gasket failure. Although this sounds scary they offer the following advice to help identify any issues:

- Lift the bonnet and look inside the header tank (located on the nearside). If there's oil inside it, the head gasket will have failed. If the level is low, there may be a leak and this may cause the engine to overheat and the head gasket to fail.
- Look inside the oil filler tank for a milky substance, which usually indicates head gasket failure.
- The cause of head gasket failure is often down to the coolant hose located under the driver's seat, which is attached to the top of the engine. It can balloon and crack, resulting in coolant loss, overheating and head gasket failure. It should be renewed if it looks at all suspicious.
- It would also be worth keeping an eye on the temperature gauge when test driving the Bongo. Make sure it does not move erratically – it should sit somewhere near the middle once the engine has been running for a while.

For a full buyers guide why not check out Practical Motorhome:

www.practicalmotorhome.com/advice/30484-mazda-bongo-camper-buyers-guide

What is a fair price?
This is a difficult question to answer as prices can vary according to age, mileage and condition and of course local supply and demand.

It is best to check local dealers as well as private sellers to establish what you believe to be a fair price for the type of Bongo you are looking for.

Try websites such as AutoTrader, Exchange and Mart, Ebay (although never buy without seeing / test driving first), Gumtree as well as your local dealer websites (a Google search should bring these up).

NOTE:

You will always pay more for a converted Bongo and if buying from a dealer.

Test Drive
ALWAYS take a test drive. Even if you know very little about Bongos you will get a feel for how it drives and will probably be able to tell if something is not quite right.

Questions
Never be afraid to ask the current owner questions or to see paperwork. If they are serious about selling their Bongo they should be more than happy to answer any questions you have. If they are vague or don't have paperwork walk away.

The following questions are a good place to start:

- Has it been recently serviced? Ask for paperwork.
- When was the cam belt changed? Is there paperwork for this?
- When was it MOT'd? Again ask to see the paperwork.
- Can the owner show you where the oil goes? And the coolant? If they can't then they won't have been checking the levels.
- Ask to see the V5 document. Check the details.
- Ask to see you how things work. You want to see the roof going up and down, internal lights, fridge etc working as well as the usual things like lights, indicators etc working.

You can find a general car buying checklist on the AA website which will help you to ask the right questions.

www.theaa.com/car-buying/used-car-inspection-checklist

Remember
If you don't feel confident, you can always pay for a professional to look over the car and test drive it for you. For example, the RAC carry out a 218 point check and road test for £99.00 (price and information correct @October 2016).

FINALLY: if you aren't sure – walk away.

Conversion Options

There are several standard conversion layouts that you will find in a Bongo.

In the diagrams below the black areas denote seating / bed and the dark grey areas are kitchen units / storage.

Rear Conversion:

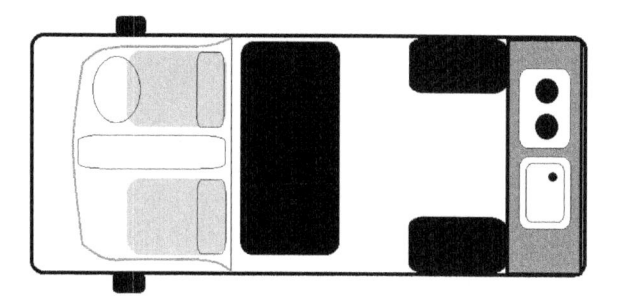

This has a kitchen unit in the boot, a backwards facing seat (this may also swivel) and two small seats / storage boxes over the rear wheel arches.

Pros: large full width seat / bed, additional dinette area

Cons: lack of headroom when cooking if you have a lifting roof (not a problem if you have a fixed high top), reduced storage and worktop space

Full Side Conversion:

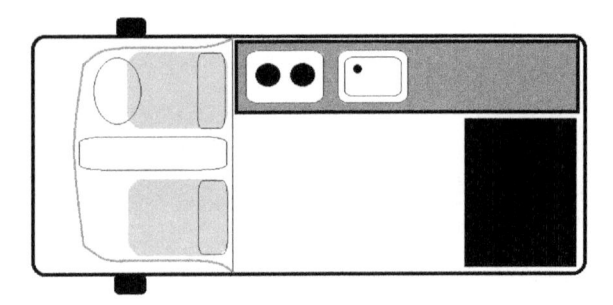

Kitchen and storage units are fitted down one side of the van and a rock 'n' roll bed is fitted at the rear.

You may find variations on this conversion with a further seat fitted behind the passenger seat but facing backwards.

Pros: extra storage space and worktop space compared to both rear and mid conversions

Cons: narrower bed than end and mid conversions

Mid Conversion:

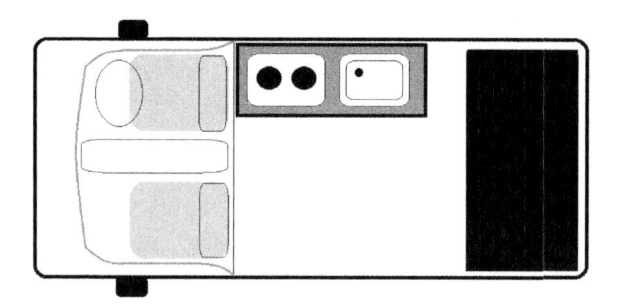

A smaller kitchen / storage unit is fitted to part of one side. The original back seats are retained to make a bed.

Pros: full width seat / bed

Cons: reduced kitchen area and storage space

The Unconverted:
You can also buy the Bongo in its original state. It will have two bench seats which can be folded down to form one large bed. This is a great way to get a feel for how you could use the Bongo before converting it.

Some original Bongos also had factory fitted kitchen units.

There are also companies that convert Bongos in slightly different ways or that may be able to modify the standard layouts to suit your needs.

Imperial Leisure Vehicles:
Based in Poole, Dorset this company have their own range of conversions and rather than using traditional wooden carcasses they use preformed fibreglass shells. These shells are curved and offer a twist on the usual mid conversion.

Take a look around my Imperial Leisure Moonfleet conversion:

www.youtube.com – search for my channel Bongo-ing Mad and check out my 'Just for Fun' playlist.

As with most things it is a matter of personal preference with each conversion option offering different benefits. There are several garages / showrooms throughout the country with various conversions on display so I would suggest visiting as many as possible to get an idea how the different spaces could work for you.

At the time of writing you can also hire Bongos so this would be a great way to try before you buy. Weekend hire starts from around £250 and you can get a week for around £600 (prices correct @ October 2016).

Professional or DIY conversion?

If you have an unconverted Bongo or your current conversion doesn't work for you it might be time for a change. However, do you take your van to the professionals or do it yourself?

You can buy self build kits on the internet along with pretty much everything you need to carry out the work yourself. However, always ensure that your insurance company will continue to insure you as some are not so keen on self builds.

You also need to ensure that you update your V5 document to show it as a Motorcaravan – check with the DVLA. This is important especially when it comes to insuring your Bongo.

Access All Areas (Getting In and Out)

Doors
All doors operate using the main key – turn clockwise to unlock and anti-clockwise to lock.

You can lock and unlock the doors from inside using the knob located on each individual door.

You can also lock the doors from the outside without using the key:

- Hold the door handle up
- Push down the knob on the inside of the door
- Shut the door
- This applies to the sliding door as well as the driver and passenger doors

Child Safety Lock – located on the edge of the sliding door

The sliding door is fitted with a child safety lock. If you set it to the lock position the door cannot be opened from the inside.

Change the lock back to unlock and the door can once again be opened from the inside.

Optional Upgrades:
You may have been lucky enough to have bought a Bongo with optional upgrades fitted and you may have some additional features....

Central Locking
If you have this option all the doors will unlock / lock when you turn the key in the driver's door.

You can also unlock / lock all doors when inside your Bongo using the internal knob.

Sliding Door
Your Bongo may have been fitted with an automatic door closure upgrade in which case the door will close automatically when half shut.

NOTE:

If you have this upgrade you must allow the door to close itself to avoid damage.

Back Door
If you have an internal back door handle fitted you will need to twist it clockwise whilst pulling it to open the door.

NOTE:

The driver's door will need to be unlocked.

Back Door Internal Light
There are 3 settings for this light. On and off which are permanent settings regardless of back door position.

If you set the button to the middle position it will turn on when the back door is open and off again when it is shut.

Front Windows
The driver and passenger door windows are electric and can only be operated when the ignition is on.

On the drivers door there are buttons for the driver and passenger's window as well as a lock switch.

The right (auto) button is for the driver's window.

When the lock switch is 'on' both the driver and the passenger can operate the passenger window. If the lock switch is moved to the 'off' position only the driver will be able to open and close the passenger window.

Driver Side Window Controls

The left switch operates the passenger window, whilst the right (AUTO) switch operates the drivers window

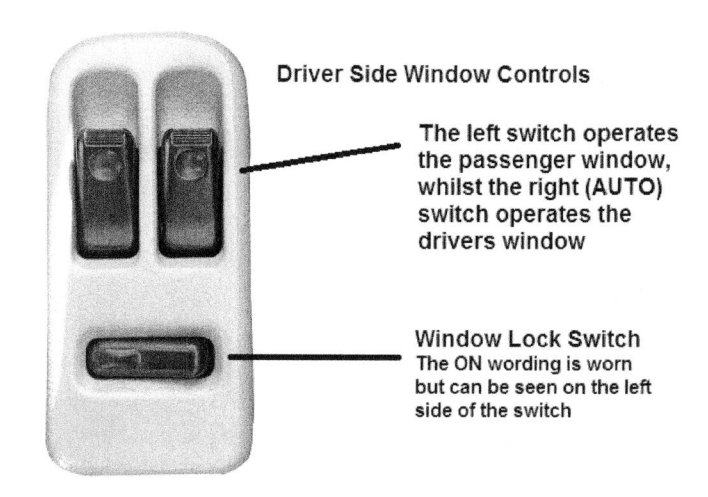

Window Lock Switch
The ON wording is worn but can be seen on the left side of the switch

Rear Windows

You will notice a small lever on the rear windows that allow you to open them slightly.

To open the window, pull the lever towards you and then push it backwards to lock it into position (the second photo shows the window in the open position). To close the window do this in reverse.

NOTE:

You are not able to open the window on the panel behind the sliding door.

The Engine
As well as being beneath the bonnet, parts of the Bongo engine are also located beneath the passenger and drivers seats.

Part 1 – The Bonnet
To open the bonnet you will need to pull the lever found in the cab to the right and below the steering wheel.

The bonnet will lift slightly allowing you room to insert your hand. You will then find a lever near the middle which you need to pull up. This will allow you to open the bonnet fully.

There is a metal stay located on the underside of the bonnet. Insert this in the hole near the front right.

When closing the bonnet always ensure it has fully clicked back into place.

Bonnet Release Lever

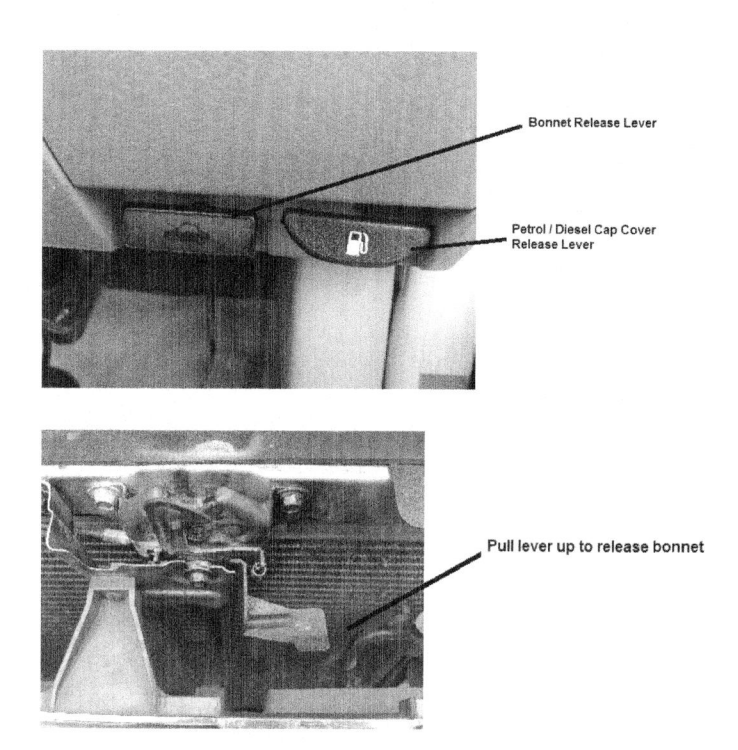

Petrol / Diesel Cap Cover Release Lever

Pull lever up to release bonnet

Part 2 – The Passenger Seat

To access the second part of the engine you will need to remove the centre console.

There are two screws that you must take out; one is located to the right side (if you have an ashtray this will need to be removed), the other is in the lift up storage section.

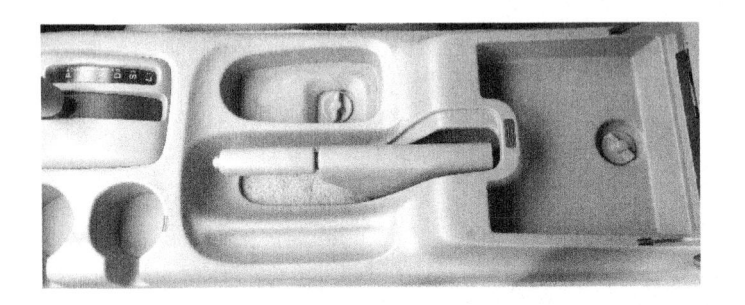

If you have a manual gearbox you will also need to loosen off the gear stick cover.

Remove the centre console by pulling it upwards.

You will now need to lift up the passenger seat.

- Slide the passenger seat as far backwards as you can. Fold the backrest down.
- Loosen the carpet from around the base of the seat and you will find three metal clips. Undo all the clips and you can now lift the seat up.

Once you have finished accessing the engine you can simply reverse the process.

The first part of my video below shows how to remove the centre console and lift the passenger seat:

www.youtube.com – Bongo-ing Mad: How to check the oil level in your Mazda Bongo.

Part 3 – The Drivers Seat
To access the third part of the engine you will need to lift the drivers' seat.

Follow the same process described above for accessing the engine beneath the passenger seat.

Filling Up
You will find the fuel cap release lever in the cab to the right and below the steering wheel next to the bonnet release lever (see above).

Optional Upgrades:
Your Bongo may be fitted with an electric sun roof. This can only be operated when the ignition is on. The switch is located next to the sun roof and is simply an on / off switch.

Getting Ready for the Off

Putting the key in the ignition – what are your options?

You will notice four options / positions:

LOCK 0
This is basically the off position. You will need to bring the key back to this position to be able to remove it. It also enables the steering wheel to lock.

When the steering wheel is locked the key will be difficult to turn. To release the lock turn the key and move the steering wheel left and right.

ACC I
This position does not start the engine but allows accessories to operate, for example the electric mirrors or windows. Do not leave the key in this position too long as it will drain the battery.

ON II
Once you have started the engine the key will return to this position. If you have stopped the engine but the key is still in the ON position it will drain the battery.

START III
Turning the key to this position will fire up the engine. Release the key and it will return to the ON position.

What's that noise?

If you leave your keys in the ignition and open the driver's door you will hear a noise. This is a reminder; this noise will only be heard when the key is in the LOCK or ON position.

Driving an Automatic

A majority of Bongos have automatic transmissions and, although simpler to drive than manual vehicles, there are a few things to remember especially if you aren't used to driving them.

As you have no clutch to worry about you only have to use your right foot to operate both the brake and accelerator pedals. Using only your right foot will avoid any confusion in an emergency.

You will notice the gear shift lever has 2 buttons on the right side. The top button is the shift lever button and this is needed to move the shift lever into certain settings (see below). The bottom button is the HOLD button and this changes how the positions detailed below work (see the Hold Mode section for full details).

You should only use the shift lever button when required to do so to avoid accidentally selecting the wrong gear / setting.

Gear Shift Lever Button

Hold Button

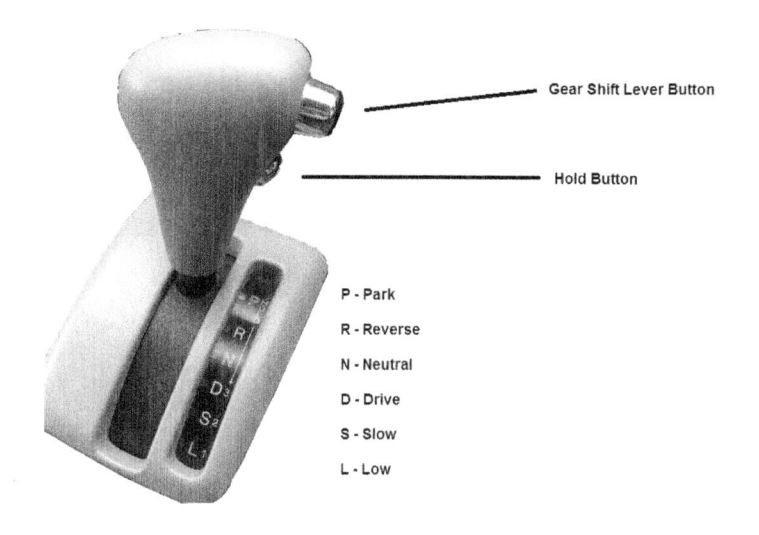

P - Park
R - Reverse
N - Neutral
D - Drive
S - Slow
L - Low

What do the letters mean?

P – Park

Park is only needed when you have reached your destination. It must only be used when the Bongo has completely stopped to avoid causing damage.

To move in or out of park you must press the shift lever button whilst also putting your foot on the brake pedal. You can move the Bongo out of park without starting the engine by moving the key to either the ACC or ON position.

R – Reverse
When you have selected reverse the Bongo will beep at you. This is a reminder / warning so you do not accidentally select reverse by mistake.

To move into reverse you must press the shift lever button whilst also putting your foot on the brake pedal.

To move from reverse to neutral you do not need to use the shift lever button.

N – Neutral
This is used only when idling for a short time, for example, when in a traffic jam or when being towed or pushed. It should NOT be used for any other purpose as you will not be able to control the speed of your Bongo.

Shift lever button not required to move into neutral.

D – Drive
The Bongo will automatically select the correct gear according to the load on the engine and your speed. For example it will automatically change into a lower gear when travelling uphill or a higher gear as your speed increases.

The Bongo has a 4 speed gearbox.

Shift lever button not required to move into drive.

Sometimes you will need to override the automatic gear selection system and select a low gear, for example when going down a steep hill. In this situation you have 2 options to 'lock' the gears (alternatively use the HOLD mode detailed below):

S – Slow Gear
The Bongo is only able to select between 1st and 3rd gears depending on speed.

Shift lever button not required to move into slow gear.

L – Low Gear
For very steep hills this selection only allows 1st and 2nd gears to be used.

To move into low gear from slow you must use the shift lever button however you DO NOT need to put your foot on the brake pedal.

You DO NOT need to use the shift lever button to move out of low gear.

NOTE:

You can also use 'S' and 'L' when driving up hills to reduce engine revs and make driving smoother.

Only use 'S' and 'L' when driving at low speeds. If used at high speeds it can cause the engine to over rev.

Hold Mode
You will notice next to the letters the word HOLD, an arrow and the numbers 3, 2, 1.

As an alternative to using 'S' and 'L' you can also use the hold mode to fix the Bongo in specific gears. This is great for situations where you need more control over your speed using the engine brake, for example, when driving down a steep hill or in icy conditions.

Your options in hold mode are:

D (3) – Fixed 3rd gear (gears will be able to change between 2nd and 3rd at low speeds)

S (2) – Fixed 2nd gear

L (1) – Fixed 1st gear

To activate the mode press the bottom hold button and move the gear shift lever to the desired gear. The HOLD light on the dashboard will be visible when the mode is selected.

To deactivate the mode press the button again. Turning off the engine will also deactivate the mode.

NOTE:

The light will be continuous. If the light on the dashboard flashes this indicates a fault.

To start the engine:
- Ensure the gear shift lever is in 'P' and the handbrake is on.
- Put your foot firmly on the foot brake.
- Turn the key in the ignition.

NOTE:

You will not be able to start the engine unless your foot is on the brake. If you have an immobiliser fitted you will also need to disable it using your fob.

The left section is an immobiliser.

Moving off:
- Keep your foot on the brake.
- Select either 'D' or 'R' as appropriate. You will need to push in the button on the side of the shift lever to do this.
- Disengage the handbrake.
- Release your foot off the brake (do this slowly as the Bongo may begin to 'creep' forwards).
- Gradually apply pressure to the accelerator.

What is 'creep'?
Bongos, like other automatics, are designed to 'creep' forwards even when the accelerator is not being pressed down. Therefore, you will need to use the foot brake or handbrake when stationary with the engine running.

Stopping in traffic:
- Apply the foot brake.
- Keep the vehicle in 'D'
- Engage the handbrake to keep your Bongo immobilised.

Overtaking / Sudden acceleration:
- Press the accelerator down hard to the floor.
- The Bongo will automatically drop down to a lower gear and increase your acceleration.
- Keep it fully pressed down until you reach the speed you need.
- Gently ease your foot up and the Bongo will select the appropriate gear.

This is known as 'Kick Down' and is an override feature forcing the gearbox to stay in a lower gear for longer thus giving you more acceleration.

Parking:
- Bring the Bongo to a complete stop.
- Keep your foot on the brake.
- Apply the handbrake.
- Select 'P'
- Release the foot brake.
- Turn off the engine.

Hill Starts:
Bongos have a feature that means you will not roll back but for steep hills it may be worth doing the following:

- Ensure the handbrake is on.
- Apply gentle pressure to the accelerator.
- The engine revs will increase (there will be an increase in noise) and you will feel the Bongo pulling forwards.
- Release the handbrake and gently increase pressure on the accelerator.

Things to remember:

- Allow longer when braking as automatic gearboxes do not respond as quickly as manuals to a reduction in pressure on the accelerator

- Always apply the handbrake or foot brake when stopping (the handbrake should be used for longer periods).

- Slow down before you reach bends and gently accelerate as you enter the bend. This will push the gearbox to select a lower gear and allow you to take the corner more slowly.

- When driving in snow and ice, to help avoid wheel spin, it helps to select a higher gear. In such situations use the HOLD mode and select either 'D' or 'S' to fix the Bongo in 3rd / 2nd or 2nd gears respectively. These gears will give you more traction when moving off or going slowly.

Switches and Buttons (What do they do?)

Adjusting the Steering Wheel
Under the steering wheel you will find a lever. Simply pull this down to adjust the height of the wheel. Once you have selected the height you want push the lever back into position.

Electric Door Mirrors
The mirror switches are located right of the steering wheel.

You can adjust each mirror individually by selecting L or R for the left or right mirrors respectively.

Push the switch to adjust the desired mirror and use the larger button to adjust the angle both up and down and side to side.

Once you have adjusted both mirrors return the L / R switch back to the middle to avoid any accidental adjustments if you catch the button.

You may also have an additional button and this is to retract the entire mirror.

One press will retract both mirrors. Just press the button again to open them out.

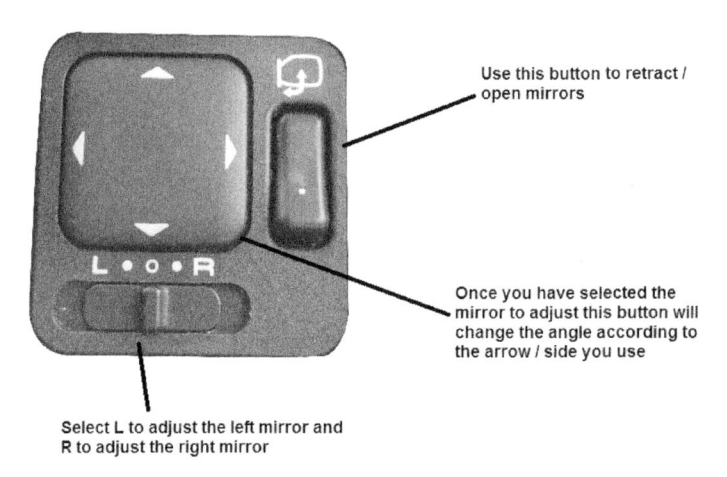

Use this button to retract / open mirrors

Once you have selected the mirror to adjust this button will change the angle according to the arrow / side you use

Select L to adjust the left mirror and R to adjust the right mirror

Lights and Wipers
You will notice that the lights / indicator and wiper stalks are positioned on the opposite sides to many European cars.

The right stalk operates the lights and indicators. The standard symbols and operation apply.

The left stalk operates the window wipers and screen wash. You have the option to adjust the speed of the wipers using the turn knob. To use the screen wash pull the stalk towards you; this will also turn on the wipers for a short time.

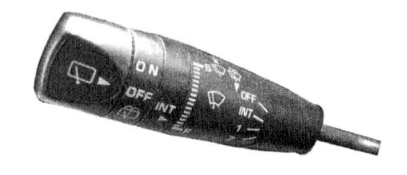

LEFT STALK
Controls window wipers and washer

The end part of the stalk is an optional upgrade so you may not have this on your Bongo. It controls the rear wiper and washer

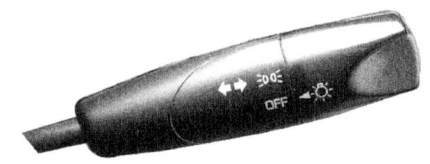

RIGHT STALK
This controls the lights and indicators

Hazard Warning Lights

The button for this standard safety feature can be found left of the steering wheel.

Air Conditioning / Fans
There are two types of air conditioning systems installed in Bongos, either manual or automatic.

Manual:
The controls in the Bongo are similar to those found in most cars / vans.
You can adjust the temperature and fan speed using the lever at the top of the control panel and the dial to the right side respectively.

The following options are available when selecting which vents will be open:

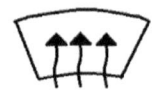

Top Row left to right: Upper Body, Upper Body / Lower Leg

Middle Row left to right: Lower Leg, Lower Leg / Defrost

Bottom Row: Defrost

NOTE:

The defrost mode is for clearing the windscreen

Upper body / lower leg mode will only work when the temperature lever is in or near the centre position

You may also choose to either re-circulate the air in the Bongo or allow fresh air in:

Left – Re-circulate Air, **Right** – Fresh Air

Re-circulating the air in the Bongo will allow it to warm up quicker. However, it will also lead to the windows steaming up if used for a long period of time.

Optional Upgrade:

Air Conditioning
You may notice an A/C button which operates the air conditioning if fitted. The air conditioning will only work when the temperature in the Bongo is high enough.

If using the air conditioning mode move the temperature lever to the left and select the fresh air setting.

You can also use the air conditioning setting to dehumidify the Bongo. Simply move the temperature lever to the right, select fresh air and select the lower leg setting.

If you move the selector to the defrost setting this will change it from dehumidify to a de-misting setting.

Automatic:
If you have an automatic air conditioner / fan fitted your control panel will be as follows:

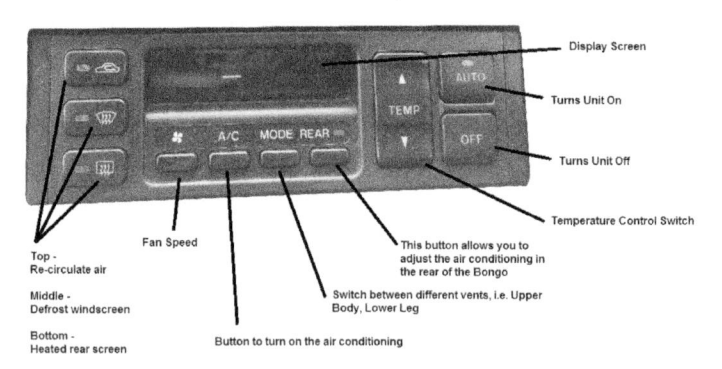

[Diagram of control panel with labels:
- Display Screen
- Turns Unit On
- Turns Unit Off
- Temperature Control Switch
- Fan Speed
- Top - Re-circulate air
- Middle - Defrost windscreen
- Bottom - Heated rear screen
- This button allows you to adjust the air conditioning in the rear of the Bongo
- Switch between different vents, i.e. Upper Body, Lower Leg
- Button to turn on the air conditioning]

Turning the heating and fans on / off:
- Press the auto switch** when selected the display light on the button will be visible
- Set the desired temperature using the up / down arrow parts of the temperature button

42

- To turn off press the off button

** the auto switch allows you to operate the following:

(1) Temperature
(2) Fan speed
(3) Air vent mode
(4) Air re-circulation
(5) Air conditioning

NOTE:

The auto mode will be stopped if you press function buttons

(1) Temperature
To adjust the temperature press the up part of the button to increase and the down part to decrease. Each press will change the temperature by 0.5 C. The maximum temperature is 32 C and the minimum 18 C.

(2) Fan Speed

This button will change the fan speed. The current speed will be shown on the display above.

(3) Air vent mode
You can select your desired mode using the MODE button. The options are:

Top Row left to right: Upper Body, Upper Body / Lower Leg

Bottom Row left to right: Lower Leg, Lower Leg / Defrost

(4) Air re-circulation

If you turn on this function you will switch from drawing in fresh air to re-circulating the air already inside the Bongo.

(5) Air conditioning
The A/C button is for turning on the air conditioning. The button will run through three options in the following order:

- A/C – normal air conditioning
- A/C ECON – economical air conditioning
- STOP (this is in Japanese) – to turn off the air conditioning

As with manual operation you have two other options:

Defrost

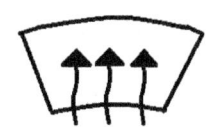

This button is for clearing a misted / fogged up windscreen. It will operate the front windscreen fans as well as the driver and passenger side vents.

Heated Rear Windscreen

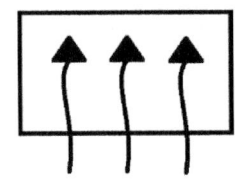

This button will operate the heated rear windscreen to clear it of mist / fog.

NOTE:

There are two temperature sensors in your Bongo if you have automatic air conditioning / fans. These are located as follows:

- Sunlight sensor – located on the driver's side, in the front corner, between the windscreen and the dashboard.

- Interior sensor – a series of small slits below the stereo / right of the glove box.

REAR

You may also have a REAR button on your display panel; this operates the air conditioning in the back of the Bongo.

- Press the button gently to turn on the air conditioning in the back.
- Press and hold the button for 2 seconds to display the rear air conditioning settings and to adjust them.

You can adjust:

- Fan speed (use the fan button)
- Air vent (use the MODE button)
- Turn on / off (use the AUTO button)

Press the REAR button again to revert back to the front controls. If you do not adjust any settings on the rear air conditioning for approximately 10 seconds the display will automatically revert back to the front controls.

NOTE:

You cannot adjust the temperature from the main control panel; this can only be done from the rear control panel.

Optional Rear Air Conditioning / Fans

If you have rear air conditioning / fans fitted you will either have a manual or automatic system.

You may have a switch fitted right of the steering wheel labelled REAR with a small light. If you do, this switch will operate the rear air conditioning.

Manual:

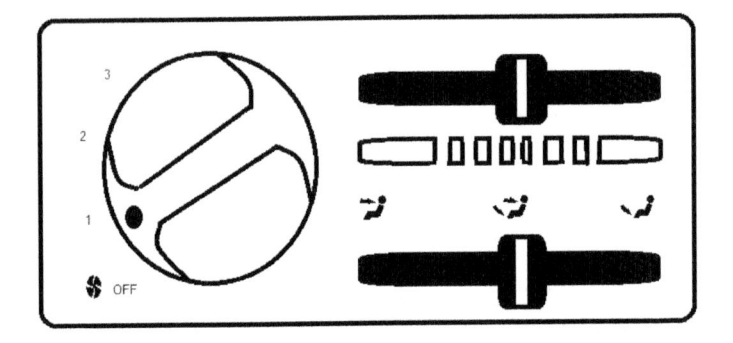

The manual controls are straight forward to use. The top slide control operates temperature, the lower slide control the vents in use and the left dial adjusts the fan speed.

Automatic:

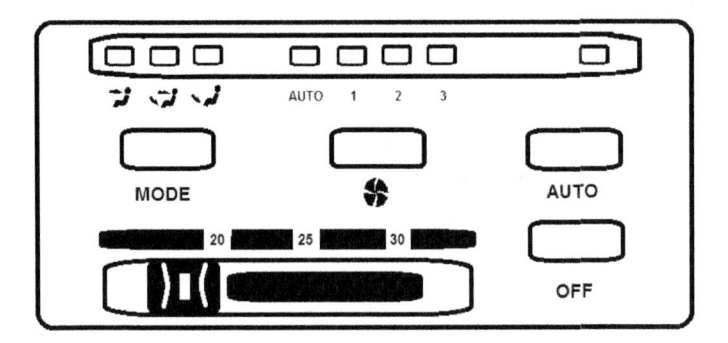

The automatic controls work in the same way the automatic front air conditioning operates.

- Press the auto switch** (the light above will now be visible)
- Set the desired temperature using the slide control at the bottom
- To turn off press the off button

** the auto switch allows you to operate the following:

(1) Fan speed
(2) Air vent mode

NOTE:

The auto mode will be stopped if you press function buttons

(1) Fan speed

This button will change the fan speed.

(2) Air vent mode

Press the button to select between upper body, upper body / lower leg and lower leg modes. See pictures above.

Optional Upgrades:
You may have additional buttons and switches to those listed above. Other factory optional upgrades include:

Warm Up System

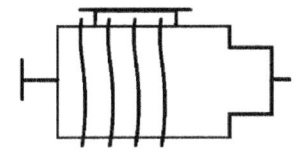

This button will be found right of the steering wheel. It allows you to shorten the warm up time in the cold weather.

To operate, start the engine and press the switch (the light on the button will come on). Press the bottom part of the switch to turn it off again.

NOTE:

If you press on the accelerator when warm up is in use it will temporarily stop the warm up function. It will start up again once you release your foot off the pedal.

Fog Light Switch

Fog lights will only work when the main headlights are on. The button is located to the right of the steering wheel in the bank of three switches.

If you do not have a factory fitted fog light switch then your Bongo should have been fitted with a rear fog light when imported into the UK as it is a legal requirement here.

If you have an after market fog light, the switch will often be located right of the steering wheel and will have a small red light which will illuminate when in use.

The symbol above may or may not be on the switch. Again, it will only work when the main headlights are on.

The right switch is an after market fog light switch.

Rear Window Wiper and Screen Wash
If you have this upgrade you will have an additional section on the end of your left (wiper) stalk. See lights and wiper section above.

Heated Rear Window

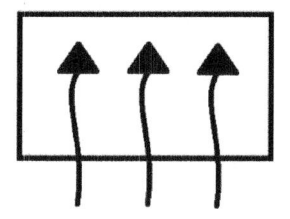

To operate simply press the button which is located in the bank of three switches left of the steering wheel: in some cases it is part of the automatic air conditioning control panel (see picture above). There is a small light to show the button is on.

Electric Blinds
If your Bongo is fitted with electric blinds you will find two sets of buttons for them:

The first set can be found left of the steering wheel (see picture). The right switch operates the driver side blinds and the left switch the passenger side blinds.

You will also find switches in the back of the Bongo. If your Bongo hasn't been converted you will find four switches; one located by each window. If your Bongo has been converted these switches may be located in different positions.

To operate the blinds you will need to make sure the ignition is set to the ON position first.

NOTE:

The blinds can be operated manually.

Electric Roof
Some Bongos are fitted with an electric roof which is very simple to operate.

To Open:
- Make sure you have parked up and applied the handbrake.
- Put the Bongo in neutral (for manual gearboxes) or P (for automatic gearboxes).

- Start the engine (opening the roof without the engine running may drain the battery).
- Press the switch (see picture) to open the roof (it will stop automatically when fully open).

- Turn off the engine
- If you have a manual gearbox select either 1st or Reverse gear

NOTE:

The warning light on the dashboard will flash when opening the roof. You will also hear a beeping noise.

To Close:
- Ensure the roof void is empty and the roof board has been lowered.

- Open a door or window to allow air to escape.
- Ensure the Bongo is either in neutral (for manual gearboxes) or P (for automatic gearboxes).
- Start the engine (see note above about engine drain).
- Press and release the Lock Cancellation Switch located on the roof (see picture).
- If you forget to press the switch you will not be able to lower the roof. After you have pressed the switch the warning light will flash and you will hear the beeping noise (if you do not close the roof during this time you will need to press the switch again). If you press the switch whilst the roof is lowering it will stop.

- Press and hold the roof switch until it stops closing (this will happen near the end of the closing procedure to enable you to check the roof void is empty).
- To finish the procedure release the switch and press it once again to fully close the roof.
- The light will go out and the beeping stop once the roof is fully lowered.
- Finally you can turn the engine off.

NOTE:

The following may indicate a fault and must be investigated:

- If you do not see the light or hear the beeping noise when the roof is being opened / closed.
- If the light or beeping continue after the roof has finished opening or closing.
- The light is not visible during operation (this may indicate a blown bulb).
- The light remains on after the engine has been started but the roof is not being opened / close.

Warning / Display Lights

The dashboard on your Bongo contains the usual things you would expect to find; the speedometer, odometer (total distance travelled (mileage)), trip meter and tachometer (engine revs) along with the water temperature gauge and fuel gauge.

Right bank of warning lights
Left bank of warning lights

Automatic Gear Display - each box corresponds to the gear selected, i.e. top = P, bottom = L

Glow plug light   Headlight light   Water temperature gauge   Fuel gauge

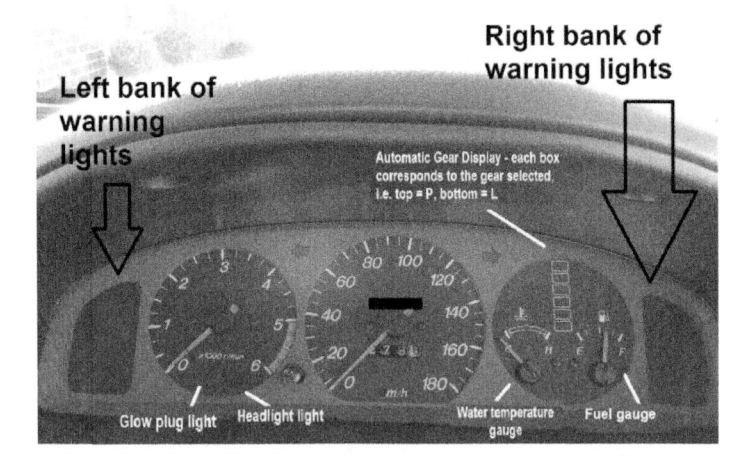

Photo shows warning and display light layout in a 2.5 Diesel automatic.

You will also find two warning / display light panels and the lights you will see on them are listed below.

If you see any of the warning lights (marked with **) lit up then you must get your Bongo checked out. It may only be a minor issue, such as a broken wire or faulty sensor but it could be something more serious that, if ignored, could cause expensive damage.

On the left side you will find:

AIR-BAG

**** Air-Bag (optional upgrade – not found on all models)**
This red warning light will appear when you turn on the ignition but will go off again after a few seconds.

If the light flashes or comes on after that time this indicates there may be a fault with the air bag system. This must be investigated.

If the light doesn't come on when you turn on the ignition this would suggest a blown bulb which will need replacing.

** Seat Belt
Below the air-bag light you will notice the seat belt light; once the driver's seat belt is fastened this light will go out.

** Door Open
This red light will illuminate if any of the doors are open. Check all doors are closed securely if it comes on.

** Brake

The brake warning light indicates a fault with the braking system and should be checked out straight away, although do check that it isn't warning that you have left the handbrake on.

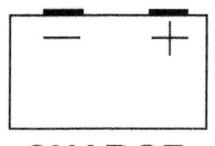

CHARGE

** Battery

The battery warning light should come on when you first turn your Bongo on and then go out after a few seconds when you have started the engine. If it doesn't go out or comes on whist driving it indicates a problem with the electrical system. This could be for a few different reasons and must be investigated to avoid damage.

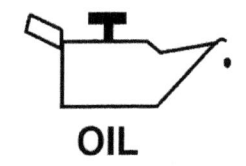

OIL

** Oil

This light will come on if the oil temperature gets too high, the level is low or oil pressure is too low.

Oil lubricates your engine and ignoring this light could lead to expensive engine damage so if it comes on, stop and phone a professional straight away.

On the right side you will find:

HOLD

Hold Mode Light (Automatics Only)
You will see this light on automatic Bongos only when you engage the Hold Mode Function as discussed in the 'Driving an Automatic' chapter.

SEDIMENT

** Sedimentation Water Tank Level (Diesel Bongos Only)
This light will come on when the water level in the sedimentation water tank exceeds the limit.

HEAT

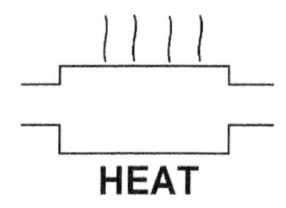

** Exhaust Temperature
This warning light indicates that the temperature of the catalytic converter is too high. If it comes on pull over as soon as possible and stop the engine. Seek professional help.

Light not found on Diesel Bongo panels.

4W ABS

** ABS (optional upgrade – not found on all models)
The ABS is a device that stops the wheels from locking when braking suddenly or on a slippery road. If the ABS fails to operate the normal braking system will kick in.

A faulty Anti-lock Braking System (ABS) should be investigated as a matter of urgency.

ROOF

** Roof Opening (optional upgrade – not found on all models)
If your Bongo is fitted with an automated lifting roof you will find this light on your dashboard. The warning light has three functions:

- To tell you that the roof is being lifted.
- You have taken the handbrake off but the roof is not fully shut.
- The roof is open and you are driving (stop and close the roof).

If the light continues to flash seek professional help.

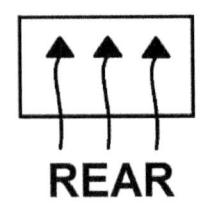

REAR

Heated Rear Window
Lights up when the rear window heater is in use.

The other lights you may see on the dashboard are:

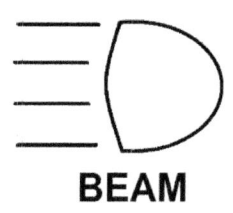

BEAM

Headlight Beam

This light will be green when the lights are on main beam. If you switch to full beam the light will turn blue.

Indicator and Hazard Lights

Left and right arrows will light up green when you indicate to turn each direction respectively. Both lights will flash if you press the hazard warning light button.

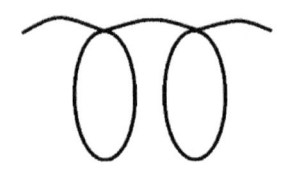

Glow plug (Diesel Bongos Only)
This light indicates that the engine is being preheated. You MUST wait for the glow plug light to go out before starting the engine.

Manuals only: Press the accelerator down firmly when turning the key. Release once the engine has started.

Quirky Bongo Bits

This chapter covers all the other quirky parts of your Bongo.

Foot Rest / Spare Seat
So what is that little folding bit behind the driver and passenger seat? Well it's a spare seat or foot rest.

- To use it as a foot rest fold it towards you.

- To use it as a spare seat, slide the front seat forward and fold the backrest down. Now simply flip the little seat backwards.

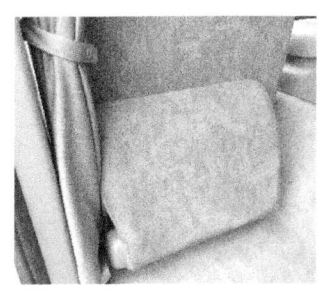

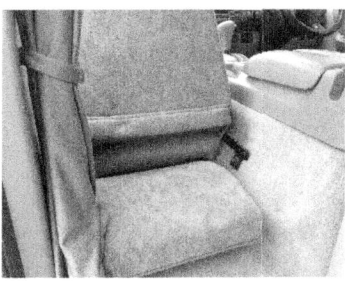

Rear Mirror
The mirror fitted on the back of your Bongo is a reversing aid.

Make sure you can view this mirror in your rear view mirror. If you look in the mirror you should be able to see your bumper and thus avoid reversing into any obstacles that you may otherwise not see.

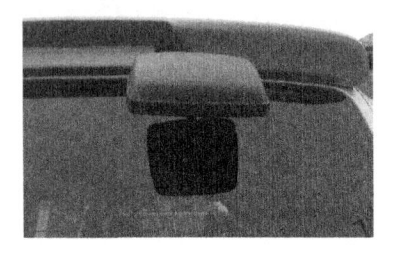

Second 12v Socket
As well as the cigarette lighter in the front of the Bongo you will find a second 12v socket in the luggage space. Just remove the cover to use (if one is fitted).
The ignition needs to be in the ACC or ON position for this socket to work.

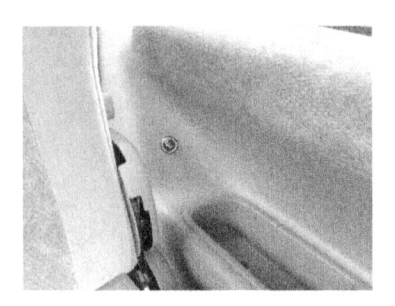

The Amazing Lifting Roof (AFT – Auto Free Top)

To give you extra space your Bongo may be fitted with a lifting roof which could be either manual or electric.

The roof is basically a tent on top of your van giving you extra space for sleeping or storage; it also gives you extra headroom. Be aware that the rooftop is only designed to hold a weight of up to 150kg.

You will also find a light in the roof void which can be set to automatically turn on and off when the rooftop is opened and closed.

If for any reason you have a problem closing the roof you can use the roof lowering kit that may be in your Bongo. If you don't have one you can purchase an 'Emergency Roof Lowering Kit' on ebay for around £9 (price correct @ October 2016). This kit is usually an exact replica of the kit that would have come with the Bongo when new.

To use the kit:
- Undo the bottom zipper and secure the tent with the belt
- Undo the top zipper then remove the net
- Lower the roof board and open the roof opening
- Attach the rope as shown in the diagram on the instructions (ensure it runs on the inside of the stay damper and that it isn't catching on the damper)
- Lay the rope on the vehicle
- Remove both motor covers while pressing the catch area
- Remove the 3 screws in each motor and then the motor itself
- Pull both sides of the rope slowly until the roof top tent closes completely (the roof will close automatically around the halfway point without pulling the rope)
- Tie the remaining rope to the grip
- Ensure you do not drive above 25 mph.

NOTE:

The kit does come with full instructions and diagrams.

The Engine
Your Bongo has a unique engine layout. It is positioned both under the bonnet and driver and passenger seats making access a bit different to standard vans and cars.

See the Access All Areas section above for full details.

Emergency Flare
Very few Bongos still have the original flare in them. They are a requirement in Japan but are often removed in this country. If you still have one it is best to remove it and dispose of it safely as they are often past their expiry date.

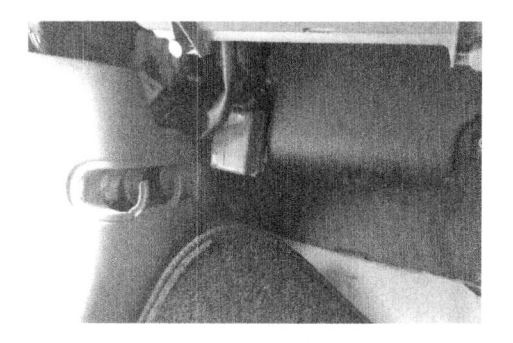

If you have a flare it will be located on the passenger side in the foot well. You can see in the picture above the space for the flare.

Accessories

There are a range of different accessories you can buy to make your Bongo life complete.

As well as the usual pots, pans and of course a kettle, you will probably want to purchase the following accessories before your first trip away:

Electric / mains hook-up cables

These usually come in either 10 or 25 meter lengths and are orange in colour for visibility. You can also buy leads with socket outlets which are for use in awnings or Bongos without a mains hook up point.

Levelling ramps and wheel grips

Most campsites are levelled to some extent but you may still find a pair of levelling ramps a really good investment to ensure you are perfectly level. Use in conjunction with a mini spirit level (see picture below) to ensure you are perfectly level.

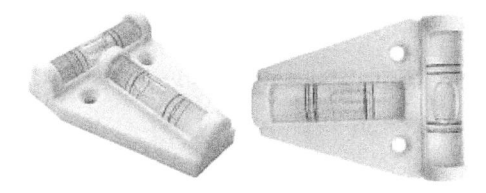

Another good investment, especially if you want to use grass pitches, is a pair of wheel grips. Use them under the drive wheels to provide grip – great in wet conditions.

Water / Waste Carriers
Your Bongo may have both fresh and waste water containers fitted or you may only have a fresh water tank.

If you have a fresh water tank fitted which cannot be removed you will need some form of carrier or hose to fill it up. There are many forms of water carriers on the market, many of which fold or collapse for easy storage. If you choose a hose ensure you buy a blue food grade hose.

If you have a sink but no on-board waste water tank you will have some form of outlet hose found under the van. You can collect waste water in any form of container ranging from a folding bucket to an off the shelf container designed for the purpose (see below).

Safety
I would highly recommend purchasing the following safety equipment for your Bongo:

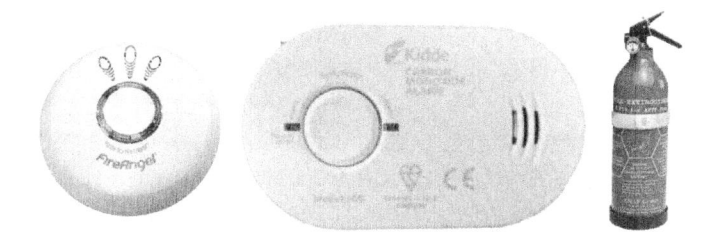

From left to right: Smoke Alarm, Carbon Monoxide Alarm, Fire Extinguisher

Fire Extinguishers
The recommended fire extinguisher for caravans / campervans etc is a powder A, B, C & electrical rated fire extinguisher. This is suitable for use on solid materials, liquids / petrol / oil, gases including propane as well as electrical fires.

Carbon Monoxide
Carbon monoxide is a silent killer, as well as fitting a suitable alarm; you should always follow these safety tips:

- **Never** take a barbecue into a tent, awning or campervan. Even a cooling barbecue produces carbon monoxide.

- **Never** use a fuel burning appliance to heat your tent or awning. Gas and kerosene heaters (unless permanently fitted in a campervan) should only be used outside. Stoves and barbecues are designed for cooking not space heating.

- **Never** run a gas, petrol or diesel generator inside your campervan, tent or awning. Make sure fumes from a generator don't blow into your or anyone else's unit either.

- **Don't** cook inside your tent or awning

- **Don't** use any other gas, charcoal, liquid or solid fuel appliances inside a tent or awning. These items need plenty of ventilation to prevent them producing carbon monoxide.

- **Always** have your campervan gas appliances serviced regularly.

Remember: test your smoke and carbon monoxide alarms every time you go away.

Travelling abroad
There are a number of different legal requirements you need to be aware of when driving in Europe.

You can buy kits that will provide you with the essentials like a disposable twin breathalyser kit (required when driving in France), beam convertors, GB stickers etc.

Always check what the latest requirements are before travelling by visiting:

www.gov.uk/driving-abroad

You may also wish to buy a two pin adaptor before travelling to Europe. Although a majority of campsites have standard three pin hook-up points some have two pin hook-ups and for those you will need an adaptor (see opposite).

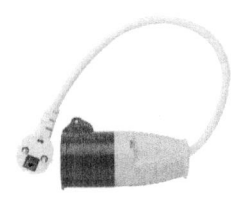

There are other considerations too varied to cover in this book, so, for full details about travelling abroad with a campervan, why not check out the Caravan Club website:

www.caravanclub.co.uk/overseas-holidays/useful-information

Other Accessories
You may also consider some of the following at some point:

Awnings – drive away, sun canopy, pop-ups, inflatable....
Bongo's are not big on internal space so many owners add space by erecting an awning.

But which type do you choose?

This, again, is personal choice but there are different factors to consider for each type.

Drive Away:

As the name suggests you put up the awning and attach it to your Bongo (normally using a figure of 8 strip attached to your Bongo's gutter rail) but you can easily detach it and drive away.

Some campsites will only allow awnings that are fitted to your outfit so this should be ok for those sites.

There are many types of drive away awning available at prices to suit most budgets.

Within the drive away range you can choose either a standard pole variety or an inflatable type.

Standard

This type of awning (two varieties pictured above) has been around for a very long time. You are normally supplied with lightweight poles and a canvas shell. You may also have fitted curtains, groundsheets and pegs.

Pros: cheaper than inflatable, easy to come by and can be very cheap second hand

Cons: more difficult and time consuming to erect especially the first time, weigh more than inflatable

Inflatable

In recent years inflatable awnings (two varieties pictured above) and tents have hit the market. These do away with standard poles and instead you inflate the structure which normally comes in one piece.

Pros: easy and speedy to erect with many taking only a couple of minutes, easy to pack away, lightweight

Cons: more expensive than standard awnings, punctures are always a possibility although the inflatable sections are usually made of a dense material

If you are not concerned about the awning being attached to your Bongo then you can consider the following:

Quechua Base Seconds

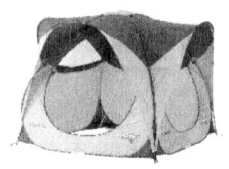

This spacious pop-up tent fits neatly next to the Bongo and, as the name suggests, can be erected in seconds.

It does not attach to the Bongo so may not be classed as an awning by some campsites so always check before you book.

Check out my video guide to see how easy it really is to set up and pack away:

www.youtube.com – Bongo-ing Mad: Quechua Base Seconds - Easy Set Up and Pack Up Guide

Tents
Alternatively you can use a standard tent to add extra space, again, just check with the campsite that this is acceptable.

Toilet tents can also be a good option if you are thinking of buying a portable toilet.

Sun Canopy
If you are looking for shelter from light rain or bright sunshine then you might want to consider a sun canopy. These come in a range of shapes but are basically a piece of tent type material that connects to your van (usually using a figure of 8 strip) and is supported by two poles and guy ropes.

They are lightweight and easy to store so could be used for day trips.

Cassette Awnings

These awnings are similar to sun canopies but are permanently fitted to your van in a cassette. They are made from a sturdy fabric and have two attached legs for support.

The most common cassette awning manufacturers are Fiamma and Thule.

You can also buy privacy rooms that attach to a cassette awning to provide additional enclosed space.

What is a figure of 8 strip?

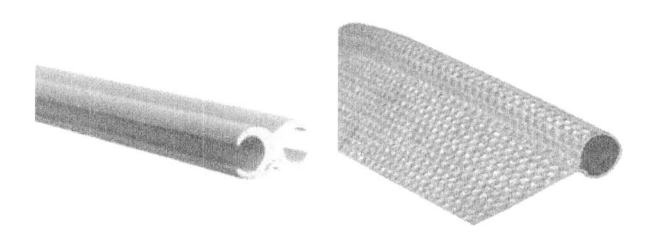

The figure of 8 strip (pictured left) enables you to attach any product fitted with a kador strip (middle picture) to your van (last picture).

You need to ensure that the kador size matches the figure of 8 size (usually 6mm or 8mm).

The figure of 8 should be attached to your gutter rail as seen in the last picture.

Cooking

You will find that Bongos don't normally come fitted with any kind of cooking facilities apart from a gas hob. If you would like to cook a wider variety of meals you may want to consider purchasing a microwave and / or mini oven.

A standard microwave is suitable for the Bongo but remember when you stay on a campsite you will have limited amps. If you are staying at a site with 16 amps you would be able to use a microwave but if the site only offers 5 or 10 amps it could well trip the circuit. Check out the calculation below.

Equally if using a microwave remember to limit the other electrical appliances being used at the same time, especially those with heating elements like kettles, electric heaters etc.

As well as a microwave you may also choose to buy a mini oven. These are cheap, very lightweight and easy to use. Again check out the calculation below to work out amp usage.

How do I know what appliances I can use on a mains hook-up?

A useful calculation is Amps equals Watts divided by Volts. Therefore, if you have a 1000 Watt kettle, and a 230 Volt supply, you must allow for 4.3 Amps to be drawn when the kettle is in use.

Barbecues

Many Bongo owners prefer to cook outdoors and you can use either a traditional charcoal barbecue or you may wish to invest in a portable gas barbecue.

A very popular range of portable gas barbecues is Cadac (pictured below).

The Cadac range come in a variety of sizes and are suitable for use with different LPG types depending on the regulator you purchase. They have a choice of cooking surfaces for both direct and indirect cooking. They also come in a carry bag for clean, easy transportation.

Curtains / Blinds and Screen Covers
You have a few choices when it comes to privacy.

Curtains:
You can buy custom made curtains from Van-X (www.van-x.co.uk) which come with curtain rails or you can make your own / have curtains made to measure. If you go down the 'making your own' route there are many rails that can be adapted to fit.

Check out my videos on fitting Van-X curtains:

www.youtube.com – Bongo-ing Mad: The Easy Way to Fit Mazda Bongo Van-X Cab Curtains

www.youtube.com – Bongo-ing Mad: The Easy Way to Fit Mazda Bongo Van-X Tailgate (rear) Curtains

Blinds:
Your Bongo will be fitted with blinds on the side windows (not the cab). You can change the material on these but I've heard it's fiddly. Alternatively, you can clean up the current material with a spray on foam carpet cleaner or steam cleaner.

For full privacy you will need to invest in either curtains or screen covers to cover the windscreen, cab windows and rear windscreen.

Screen Covers:
If you intend to use your Bongo in the colder months or you prefer not to fit curtains you can buy screen covers. There are two types; those that fit on the inside and those that fit around the outside.

Internal covers will provide some insulation and privacy. They usually fit to both the front windscreen, side cab windows and rear windscreen with suction cups. You can use these in addition to curtains for added warmth.

External covers are usually only available for the front windscreen (they also cover the side cab windows). They provide greater insulation and stop condensation on the front windows. They usually have a piece of material that sits over the driver and passenger doors to pull them taught. Again they can be used in conjunction with curtains for added warmth.

Portable Toilets

As your Bongo doesn't have any onboard facilities you may wish to purchase a portable toilet like the Thetford Porta Potti Qube 145.

It is the perfect addition to any Bongo and, measuring only 330mm (H) x 383mm (W) x 427mm (D) and weighing 3.6kg (empty), the Thetford Qube 142 is easy to carry even when full. The waste holding tank capacity is 12L and the flush water tank holds 15L.

Some conversions have cupboard space for small portable toilets or you can buy toilet tents to house your toilet once you have pitched up.

Check out my video to find out more:

www.youtube.com – Bongo-ing Mad: How your Thetford Porta Potti (portable toilet) works

Mattresses
You may wish to purchase mattresses for both the roof bed and your standard bed. Roof mattresses are often tailor made and come in sections for easy storage.

These are easily obtainable and make for a much more comfortable nights sleep.

Solar Panels
If you plan to wild camp or stay on campsites without paying for an electric hook-up you may wish to invest in solar panels. They continue to top up your leisure battery enabling you to power your fridge and other 12v accessories for as long as you need.

There are a wide range available and can be fitted by a competent DIY installer.

The Folding Revolution
When space is tight there is nothing better than an item that folds… and there are plenty to choose from:

From folding kettles, saucepans, washing up bowls, buckets to lanterns there is a whole world of folding camping accessories out there.

Frequently Asked Questions

What are the dimensions of a Bongo?

Length – 4.58m (15')

Width – 1.69m (5'6")

Height – 2.09m (6'10")

Gross Vehicle Weight – 2260kg

What should the tyre pressures be?

The recommended tyre air pressures (noted in the manual) are:

Standard tyres

Front 195 / 70 R15 92S
2WD 180 kPa (26 psi)
4WD 200 kPa (29 psi)

Rear 215 / 65 R15 96S
240 kPa (34.8 psi)

Emergency Spare T135 / 90 D15
420 kPa (60.9 psi)

These pressures are for an unconverted Bongo.

Other sources suggest 30 psi for the front tyres, 34 psi for the rear tyres and 60 psi for the emergency spare.

It is worth remembering that the pressures should be increased if you have a converted Bongo and forums suggest a number of owners use 40 psi for all tyres. If in doubt contact your local tyre dealer / fitter who should be able to advise you further.

How do I check / change the oil?
To access the dipstick you need to access the engine beneath the passenger seat – see the Access All Areas section above for detailed instructions.

You can also check out my video on You Tube:

www.youtube.com – Bongo-ing Mad: How to check the oil level in your Mazda Bongo

What oil should I use?
It is recommended that you use 10W-30 semi synthetic oil in your Bongo (both petrol and diesel models).

What coolant / anti-freeze should I use?
Anti-freeze is essential to keep your Bongo running smoothly during the winter months. It lowers the freezing point of the water in your Bongo's engine cooling system, preventing the water from freezing when it gets cold.

Anti-freeze also increases the boiling point of engine coolant to prevent it from overheating, protecting your engine from corrosion and aiding heat transfer.

You can use either red or blue coolant / anti-freeze in your Bongo but you must never mix the two. Therefore, if you currently have blue continue using blue.

This yellow warning sticker on the underside of a Bongo bonnet states that a high quality Ethylene Glycol Anti-Freeze Coolant for Aluminium Engines should be used.

What is the difference?
Blue anti-freeze has a 2 year life span whereas red anti-freeze will last up to 5 years.

Most Bongo forums suggest that red antifreeze is better.

If you wish to change the anti-freeze / coolant in your Bongo then you need to drain the system before refilling with your preferred choice.

Coolant alarms – do I need one?
As discussed in the buying section at the beginning of the book, unfortunately, Bongos have a reputation for head gasket failure caused by overheating and often an underlying coolant leak.

The temperature gauge can often be a little unreliable when it comes to detecting such problems and most Bongo owners invest in a coolant alarm which picks up on any overheating much sooner.

Coolant alarms are readily available and can be fitted by anyone competent in DIY.

Most forums recommend owners fit one for peace of mind.

Where is my jack and spare wheel?
You will find your jack, jack handle, wheel nut wrench and wheel stopper stored in the small compartment set into your side steps (see pictures).

To access simply turn the knob and slide the cover to the right.

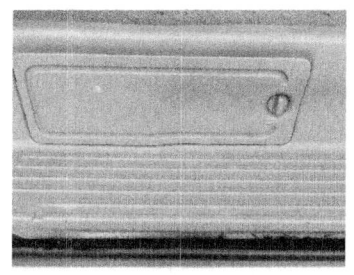

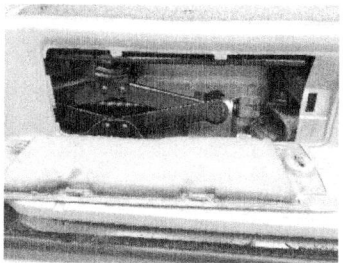

The spare tyre is located under the Bongo (see picture). This may be an emergency tyre which should only be used to take you to the closest garage / tyre fitter.

Spare Wheel   Open tailgate to see point to insert jack

To access the tyre:
- Insert the jack lever into the opening (see picture above).
- Attach the jack handle to the lever and turn it anti-clockwise (this will lower the tyre).
- Remove the hook.

To replace the tyre reverse the access instructions remembering to turn the lever clockwise.

Where are my fuses?
Bongos have two fuse boxes: one located right of the steering wheel and one located under the bonnet.

Each fuse box should list which fuses are present although this may be in Japanese.

Photo shows fuse panel located in the cab. You can see the fuse amps but unfortunately the description is in Japanese.

Photo shows fuses located under the bonnet. These have an English description.

If changing a fuse, ensure the ignition is in the LOCK position and always replace it with the same amp fuse.

If you replace a fuse and it blows immediately this may indicate a more serious problem and you should seek help.

Full details and diagrams can be found online. Websites such as Bongo Fury have many technical diagrams available for members. Membership is currently £13.00 for a basic membership (price correct @ November 2016).

LPG - What is the difference between Butane and Propane?

Butane and Propane have slightly different properties, the most important being the boiling point at atmospheric pressure.
In other words, the temperature at which it changes from being a liquid to being a gas. Butane will only readily change to a gas above 0 C, so is generally suitable for use in spring to autumn. Propane, on the other hand, will become a gas down to -40 C and therefore can be used in winter, or all year round if desired. In UK Propane is generally sold in red cylinders, Butane in blue; however, BP manufacture a lightweight propane cylinder which is green.

Where are my towing points?

You have two towing hooks located at the front of the Bongo:

Two towing hooks are located at the front of the Bongo

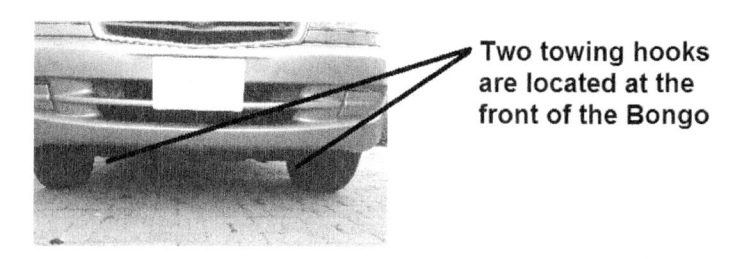

And one towing hook is located at the rear:

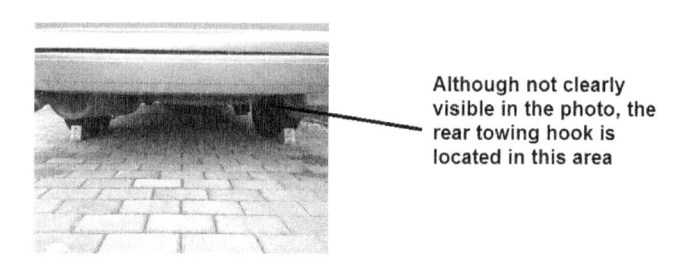

Although not clearly visible in the photo, the rear towing hook is located in this area

Should I name my Bongo?

Of course; it is traditional to name your Bongo and the majority of owners seem to go for a name beginning with 'B'.

Use your imagination and go for it.

What now?

facebook

Check out my Facebook page **Bongo-ing Mad**

My You Tube channel also has lots of helpful videos so why not subscribe – **Bongo-ing Mad**

I upload new videos regularly so check out my channel for new content.

There are lots of other groups on Facebook for Bongo owners so why not check them out:

- Mazda Bongo Owners
- Mazda Bongo

Plus many local groups so why not see if there is one in your area.

Or visit these websites:

Bongo Fury - http://igmaynard.co.uk/

The Bongo Forum –
http://www.bongoforum.me.uk/

The above is a new website address, for old posts you can visit the old site www.bongoforum.co.uk

There are other websites out there so why not see what you can find.

For more general information you can also visit:

The Caravan Club

www.caravanclub.co.uk/advice-and-training/

The Camping and Caravanning Club

http://campingandcaravanningclub.co.uk/helpandadvice/

Both websites are well worth looking at and there are benefits for joining both including monthly magazines, reduced pitch fees on club sites etc.

Note from the Author

As a fellow Mazda Bongo owner I have compiled this book to try and answer some of your Bongo / Freda questions and help you understand a bit more about your beloved Bongo.

I am not a mechanic and much of the knowledge I have is from driving my Betty Bongo and discovering all her quirky bits.

I hope the book helps you learn more about your Bongo and to bring even more joy to your adventures together.

Remember:
Camp more, explore more, enjoy more – live life!
See you soon
Claire

E&OE

Printed in Great Britain
by Amazon